Miniatures

DAVID CREGAN

First published in 1970
by Methuen & Co Ltd
11 New Fetter Lane London EC4

printed by the Redwood Press Ltd
Trowbridge Wiltshire

AUTHOR'S NOTE

This play was given two English Stage Society Sunday
Nights in 1965, was later televised by the Stables
Theatre Company for Granada Television, and was then
performed live by them in the Stables Theatre in Manchester. It has therefore undergone several changes
apart from those common to most plays, especially
early ones, in their passage from desk to performance.
The present version is a combination of the first stage
version, the television version, and one or two new
bits. I hope it is the most satisfactory version so far.
It requires either a composite set or no set at all for
its performance. It might be worth mentioning that the
later parts of Scene Eight in Act Two between Janet
and David can be performed as if walking down the
school corridors, the last part with Reg being done in
Reg's office.

I should like to thank Gordon McDougall and the Stables
Theatre Company for rescuing the play when all, in-
cluding me, had forgotten it. But most of all I should
like to thank Donald Howarth for giving it not only its
first performance, but also more or less its first shape,
carved from the flabby condition in which he found it.
His production was a very happy one, and in gratitude
I would like to dedicate this version, still very close
to the one he largely helped construct, to him.

Miniatures was first performed in a production-without-décor by the English Stage Society on Sunday, May 2nd 1965, at the Royal Court Theatre, with the following cast:

JOE JOHNSON, Head of Music		Nicol Williamson
MIKE MACALPINE, Languages		Jon Laurimore
SIMPSON	Sixth Formers	Richard James
JANET		Jane Birken
SECRETARY		Mary Macleod
A SMALL BOY		Brian Boulton
RAYMOND KNALL, English		Roddy Maude-Roxby
REG PARSONS, Deputy Head-master, Head of History		Lindsay Anderson
AMY SELKIRK, Senior Mis-tress, Head of Languages		Irene Richmond
DAVID CORNWALLIS, Head, master		George Devine
JOYCE PINNINGTON, English		Anna Gilchrist
JOHN HARCOURT, Head of English		Graham Crowden
SHEILA, Games		Jane Murdoch
HARRY CLOPTON, Head of Science		Bryan Pringle
TEA LADY		Miriam Brickman
OTHER TEACHERS		Vernon Dobtcheff
		Anne Jameson
		Sidney Johnson
		Brenda Kempner
		Julia McCarthy
		Raul Ostos
		Anthony Roye
		June Sylvaine
		Anthony Watkin

Directed by Donald Howarth

The action takes place in large modern school buildings.

Miniatures was subsequently presented at the Stables Theatre Club, Manchester, on May 21st, 1969, with the following cast:

JOE JOHNSON	John Shrapnel
MIKE MACALPINE	Brian Smith
SIMPSON	Richard Howard
JANET	Carla Challenor
SECRETARY	Jacqueline Da Costa
A SMALL BOY	Mark Lilley
RAYMOND KNALL	Richard Wilson
REG PARSONS	Ewen Solon
AMY SELKIRK	Zoe Hicks
DAVID CORNWALLIS	John Byron
JOYCE PINNINGTON	Fiona Walker
JOHN HARCOURT	Andre Van Gyseghem
HARRY CLOPTON	Paul Williamson

Directed by Gordon McDougall and John Downie from the television production by Peter Plummer

Act One

SCENE ONE

JOE JOHNSON's classroom, the music room. JOE is listening to a record player.

SIMPSON and JANET, two sixth-formers, are at the door, waiting for him to speak.

JOE: What d'you want, Simpson?

SIMPSON: A violin lesson, sir.

JOE: There aren't any violin lessons. They've stopped.

SIMPSON: Why's that?

JOE: You'd better sit down.

JANET: Must we?

JOE: Yes.

    (The music goes on and they all listen to it.

    Through the window comes the voice of MIKE MACALPINE.)

MIKE (unseen): Anything in assembly?

    (Silence from JOE.)

    Do I have to go to the common room to find out?

    (Silence from JOE.)

JANET: Mr Macalpine's calling, sir.

MIKE (unseen): Joe Johnson stinks!

SIMPSON: I think you're wanted, Mr Johnson.

JOE: Please pay attention. This is the Utrecht Te Deum and Jubilate.

    (They continue listening to the music which has never stopped. MIKE bursts in.)

MIKE: You want to waste my time?

SIMPSON: There was nothing in assembly, sir.

MIKE: Thank you. Man's effectiveness is always impeded by trivia, Simpson.

SIMPSON: Yes, sir.

JANET: May I go back to maths, please, sir?

(JOE is taking off the record.)

JOE: No, this is your violin lesson.

JANET: I don't like the violin, Mr Johnson.

JOE: We were listening to the Utrecht Te Deum and Jubilate. Will you stay?

MIKE: I'm sorry. I interrupted you.

JOE: Or will you go to your class?

MIKE: I'm late for it already. As a pretty girl, Janet, you should like music.

JANET: Yes, sir.

SIMPSON: May we have some Mozart, please?

JOE: Certainly, Simpson.

SIMPSON: Thank you, sir.

(JOE puts on the clarinet concerto by Mozart.)

MIKE: The point about human beings is that they can learn.

JANET: That's why I want to be a teacher, sir.

May I go back to maths, please? I loathe Mozart, actually.

(JOE takes off the Mozart.)

I know his appeal is universal. I'm a freak, aren't I?

MIKE: What can one say?

SIMPSON: Mr Johnson teaches us a bit at this point.

(JOE puts on the slow movement.)

JOE: Janet, have you ever let yourself go? Are you in love? Do you like anyone so much that when you think of them your tummy falls out?

JANET: As a matter of fact –

JOE: That's letting yourself go. That's when the demands

of your imagination are at their strongest and you're in danger of doing uncivilised things.

JANET: Last time you said Mozart was the most civilised composer there is.

JOE: You must let the notes come out at you and tug at you. Don't try to think. Just let the sounds ravish you.

(JOE stares ahead.)

JANET: It's no good, sir.

(Silence from JOE.)

Sir?

(Silence from JOE.)

Sir!

MIKE (listening hard): Sh.

JANET: I want to go back to maths.

MIKE: Go on, then.

JANET: Simmy?

SIMPSON: No.

(JANET goes. The others all listen. JOE suddenly produces a fountain pen from his pocket.)

JOE: This is yours, I think, Simpson.

SIMPSON: I lost it ages ago.

JOE: I've been meaning to give it back to you. I don't quite know why.

(SIMPSON receives this pen back. Music goes on.)

JOE: You don't prefer maths to music, then, Simpson.

MIKE (listening intently): Sh.

JOE: Actually, things don't come much better than maths.

MIKE: Quiet!

JOE: Clear, visionary, hard.

MIKE: For God's sake shut up.

JOE: Maths has nothing hallucinatory about it, Simpson. You should enjoy it.

MIKE (heading for the record player): If you're going to talk I'm leaving you.

JOE: It might be just as well. Your class will be wondering where you are.

MIKE: You're in a stupid mood this morning, aren't you?

JOE: Not that I'm aware of.

MIKE: Letting your class walk out on you, talking through Mozart. You're a bloody philistine. Oh...

(In taking off the record he completely removes the record player head.)

JOE: Ah. That's that, then. It's over.

MIKE: What is?

JOE: The record player. It's complete now.

(To SIMPSON):

Maths, too completes itself, like all the classical arts. It has its own energy.

(He closes the lid of the record player and it comes off in his hand.)

You see? The record player is complete, Simpson. Over. Energy all gone. Finished.

(He hands the lid to SIMPSON.)

Will you take this?

MIKE: Aren't you going to mend it?

JOE: It can't be done. It's finished. You can't mend a symphony. You can't mend a record player.

MIKE: That's a very doubtful comparison.

JOE: No.

MIKE: Yes.

JOE: No.

SIMPSON (to JOE): Are you all right, sir?

JOE: Yes. I'm perfectly in control. It isn't true that the

scientific method isn't passionate. It's Shelley and Tchaikovsky who aren't passionate, since they have merely accepted well-known positions and postured about them. There are times, Simpson, when you seem to be a romantic.

SIMPSON: I wouldn't say that, sir.

JOE: However, I've recently had hopes that you'll make a true classicist eventually.

SIMPSON: Thank you, sir.

MIKE: I'll have the lid, Simpson.

JOE (seizing it): No. This lid has to go to Simpson. Now it has become detached, there's no other way for it to fulfil itself.

MIKE: What about the record player?

JOE: It had to play music, but now it can't do that because you've broken it.

MIKE: I can't let you give bits of it away.

JOE: And so we all move darkly towards our destinies. Simpson, take the lid.

(SIMPSON does so.)

MIKE: You're mad as a hatter, aren't you?

JOE: Are you going to teach today?

MIKE: I thought you said you had a violin lesson?

JOE: The violins are not to be played on by learners.

MIKE: Learning is the point about human beings. You know that, Joe. Joe? What is it?

JOE: I'm not mad, I'm hanging on in the face of grave difficulties.

(To SIMPSON):

Keep that lid and go.

SIMPSON: Wouldn't you like to re-think everything, sir?

JOE: There's nothing to re-think. I've come to the end and that's final.

(He calmly throws the record player out of the window.)

MIKE (eventually): Well, I don't know.

JOE: We've passed the point of decision. Your life in this school, Simpson, will now complete itself without further effort. You can do nothing about it. That is morality.

MIKE: Morality?

JOE: Mathematics, classicism.

MIKE: Don't be ridiculous. Morality, Simpson, is a question of striving.

JOE: There are hard, stony little things in life, Simpson and you should collect them. Mozart. Mathematics. Do you hear me, Simpson.

SIMPSON: Yes, sir.

JOE: Morality is merely that. The hard stony little things.

MIKE: Morality is the intention to do better.

JOE: There you are, Simpson. Take your choice.

SIMPSON: Last night I went home with Janet and we undressed together. We played ludo.

MIKE: Ludo?

SIMPSON: Yes.

MIKE: You're a poseur, Simpson.

SIMPSON: We enjoyed it, sir.

JOE: It sounds classical. Mere enjoyment, however, isn't enough. Unless you were passionately involved by the ludo, such a scene sounds ridiculously affected.

(THE SCHOOL SECRETARY appears at the door.)

SECRETARY: Mr Macalpine.

MIKE: What?

SECRETARY: I think you're supposed to be teaching 3B.

MIKE: Well?

SECRETARY: You're not doing it.

MIKE: There are more important things in life than 3B.

SECRETARY: I'll tell them you're coming, then.

(She goes.)

MIKE: Without me, Simpson, 3B would know no French. That's morality.

(MIKE goes out.)

JOE: I really think that's all Simpson.

SIMPSON: It won't be easy, explaining this, sir.

(Indicating the lid.)

JOE: No, it won't. You'll just have to do the best you can.

SIMPSON: Yes, sir. Good morning, sir.

JOE: Good morning, Simpson.

(The bell rings, JOE hums the slow movement of the Mozart. JOE goes into his store cupboard and closes the door.)

SCENE TWO

RAYMOND crosses the stage towards the DEPUTY HEAD-MASTER's office. He passes SIMPSON carrying the record player lid. He registers mild surprise but continues on his way. In the DEPUTY HEADMASTER's room REG is in the process of taking all the notices off one notice board and putting them on another. RAYMOND lifts his hand to knock. As he does so REG speaks.

REG: Come in, Raymond.

(Surprised, RAYMOND goes in.)

RAYMOND: How did you know I was there?

REG: Your feet.

RAYMOND: Do they smell?

REG: Your gait has certain distinctive qualities which are easily recognisable. A shuffle is the most obvious singularity, I think, associated with you.

RAYMOND: I wouldn't say shuffle was the word. Neither glide nor lumber, but something in between.

REG: A fast amble.

RAYMOND: Or slow trot. I rather like the word claudicate, myself.

REG: I don't think I know the word claudicate, Raymond.

RAYMOND: First time I heard it was from the Master on a genuine academic summer's afternoon, gazing across the court at the head porter, Horrabin, typical head porter, an extraordinary facility for remembering people's names, my father's for instance, and I think my uncle's, Uncle George, that is, not Uncle Timothy, who's red brick, family skeleton.

(He chuckles.)

Anyway, there was Horrabin, a big box under his arm, Chateau Yquem for the college cellars or beer for the captain of boats

(He chuckles.)

Anyway, this was the third crate, and old Horrabin, who must've been seventy-five at least, since Uncle George was eighty, which actually makes him...

(He screws up his eyes.)

REG: Did something eventful happen, Raymond?

RAYMOND: Eighty-two, I suppose. Oh, yes. Something happened. There he was, third crate, coming across the quad, hot summer's day, Master and I watching. You can visualise it. 'Horrabin,' said the Master as he passed. 'Yes, Master,' 'D'you know what you are?' 'No, Master.' 'You're a claudicator,'

(He chuckles.)

And then we walked away.

(He chuckles.)

To claudicate means to limp, after the Emperor Claudius.

REG: Did you want to see me, Raymond?

RAYMOND: Yes, Reg, I did want a quiet word with you. Gowns.

REG: Joe Johnson wasn't wearing his today.

RAYMOND: You noticed?

REG: Of course.

RAYMOND: Well?

REG: What?

RAYMOND: School policy. It ought to be made clear that we all wear gowns all the time.

REG: Begin as we mean to go on.

RAYMOND: All or nothing.

REG: Well, Raymond, it's the Headmaster who has the final decision in matters of this kind.

RAYMOND: Ah. Now. You have the Headmaster's ear.

REG: Yes.

RAYMOND: His confidence.

REG: Perhaps.

RAYMOND: Or else he wouldn't have made you Senior Master.

REG: Deputy Head.

RAYMOND: Over Amy Selkirk.

REG: Senior Mistress.

RAYMOND: You appreciate distinctions.

REG: Naturally.

RAYMOND: So. Our cause is not without hope.

REG: Our cause, Raymond?

RAYMOND: Is our academic status to be recognised or is it not?

REG: Of course.

RAYMOND: Then gowns have got to be worn!

REG: Well, now, let it be given that our authority is the

sine qua non, the without which nothing of school life.
It then follows that such authority must lie on one
side of the desk only.

RAYMOND: Agreed.

REG: But it may be said, and by the Headmaster, that
the wearing of gowns is not authority but mummery,
and that as intelligent and more than intelligent
adults, we should eschew such medieval theatricalia.

RAYMOND: He used those words?

REG: Would I have made them up?

RAYMOND: I'm flabbergasted.

REG: An archaism like the gown –

RAYMOND: Archaism!

REG: The Headmaster's word, Raymond, not mine. As
an historian I find it distasteful.

RAYMOND: The gown is the continuing symbol of the
intellect.

REG: Would you say that all the intellectuals of your
acquaintance were united in support of gown? Would
flock, as it were, to the gown if it were threatened?

RAYMOND: Certainly.

REG: Some might. Some might not. For instance, common
room –

RAYMOND: Exactly! Our common room has intellectuals
with gowns, and non-intellectuals without.

REG: The Head might ask you whether if Joe Johnson
suddenly took to the gown he would thereby become
an intellectual.

RAYMOND: Of course.

REG: Pardon?

RAYMOND: It's clear enough, I should've thought. He
would've changed his mind, and intellect is a portion
of the mind. What would he have changed it to? To
the attitude of the gown, and intellect being largely a
question of attitude, the whole tone of Joe Johnson
would undergo a change. In fact, tone is what we need,
Reg, because this school is desperately lacking in tone.

REG: What?

RAYMOND: To use your own term, it is a cattle market.

REG: I hope you have weighed your words carefully, Raymond, for I would find them very disturbing if they were spoken lightly. There are certain sections of the school I would designate and have designated a cattle market, but our colleagues in common room are a carefully selected body of men and women. The Headmaster has been fortunate, I would say, in his selection of many of them. Exceptionally fortunate, I would say, Raymond.

RAYMOND: Clopton, Macalpine, Johnson?

REG: Willing men, lively men, Raymond.

RAYMOND: Dissenters.

REG: Men of ideas.

RAYMOND: Their attitude, Reg.

REG: Not unproductive.

RAYMOND: Damn that, Reg! Where are their gowns, their honours, their hard won signs of ratiocinative dexterity? We must drum them into line, Deputy Headmaster, and we must do so before defection spreads and you yourself decide to shed your vestments.

REG: Raymond!

RAYMOND (marching about): Yes, Reg, you! I speak not in jest.

REG: Who's of our faction?

RAYMOND: Some of the arts. Most of the sciences are against us.

REG: Languages?

RAYMOND: Amy Selkirk and Macalpine both against.

REG: And of course, the Headmaster is against us.

RAYMOND: Oh, yes. As I watch him going down the corridor like the chief executive in a garment factory, I realise with a sense of horror that there he goes, our Headmaster, as you say. There's no pleasure, Reg, in watching him and knowing that.

You don't feel subsumed into the academic life by a lounge suit. I long to see him passing down the corridors as if they were cloisters, asserting the calm of knowledge, the supremacy of letters, illuminating with every step the academic quaintness and charms, the love of learning for its own dear sake. But no! He never does. The time has come to make it absolutely clear that we expect the badges of respect upon our Head, even though he is a scientist.

REG: A dinner party has been in the wind for some time, now. Perhaps I could persuade Ethel to choose with care. Harcourt, ourselves and the Head.

RAYMOND: Would he come?

REG: Why not? He wouldn't know our purpose.

RAYMOND: I don't suppose the issue will go further?

REG: Raymond?

RAYMOND: The Governors?

REG: Mr Knall?

RAYMOND: It is unusual to have a scientist as Head. Historians of course –

REG (interrupting): We're very fortunate in our Head, Mr Knall, very fortunate indeed, and I find your remarks very disturbing. We have a loyalty to the Headmaster, a loyalty to the school, and yes, even a loyalty to our pupils that it would be highly irresponsible to disavow. Any question which brings criticism upon the person of the headmaster it is your duty to condemn. Publicly. In common room, of course, it's rather different, for it is a sacred principle of teaching and one that I am constantly affirming that whatever is done in common room is done in camera.

RAYMOND: Then between us may I say –

REG: You may not. It is my opinion, and I will not change it, that we are very fortunate indeed to have David Cornwallis as our Headmaster.

RAYMOND: Yes.

REG: I find your inferences disturbing.

RAYMOND: Yes.

REG: Everything is for common room to decide even the question of gowns.

(They stare at each other. The bell goes.)

You must believe that, Raymond, or I shall wonder what sort of a person I am talking to.

RAYMOND: Yes.

REG: My job is simply to discern the shall we say disturbances of pattern in common room, not to govern it. To chart the disturbances, perhaps to report them. Even, if it seems correct, to calm them.

RAYMOND: Ah!

REG: No! I am simply the buffer, the meat, as it were, in the sandwich, noticing a trend here, putting a point there. I am the shock absorber, the oil on the water, the headmaster's crutch, common room's line of communication. If I went, Raymond, this school would suffer what one might justifiably refer to as a rupture. And in this question of gowns common room is sacred, and common room in camera must decide.

(He leans forward.)

But Raymond, it must decide correctly. How, Raymond, how?

(Smiling):

Well, Deputy Headmaster, we could begin with a review of the other side. First, Johnson.

(They lean towards each other.)

SCENE THREE

The HEADMASTER's office. DAVID CORNWALLIS, who is distinguished and modish, and AMY SELKIRK, who is gowned and forty-five, and JOHN HARCOURT who is the same though thinner, and JOYCE PINNINGTON who is thirty and ungowned, are all near a large set of plans on the HEADMASTER's desk.

DAVID: They start tomorrow.

JOYCE: Oh!

DAVID: It's become a fetish. Since the school opened I've only had one thought, and that is to bring the buildings as up to date as they should've been when we started. This means we're now only ten years out of date.

JOYCE: Splendid!

DAVID: Thank you, Joyce. It's a modest achievement, I suppose, but something.

HARCOURT: I wonder, a small point, Headmaster, but one I ought to put to you, since this block is separated from the main one, ought there not to be facilities for waterproofs and wellingtons and so forth?

DAVID: Can't you see them?

HARCOURT: Not immediately.

AMY: Lavatories. Perhaps they're there.

DAVID: No, no. Not enough room.

(They all peer closely.)

HARCOURT: Are they in the old corridor?

DAVID: That's coming down.

JOYCE: There's this corner behind the prep rooms.

AMY: Wasn't there to be an extension to the changing rooms?

HARCOURT: Where?

(They all peer.)

JOYCE: Perhaps they're just behind the doors. Just – behind the doors – in the classrooms. Behind the doors.

DAVID: We're being absolutely foolish. Let me look properly.

(They move away and leave DAVID in charge of the sheet.)

JOYCE: I mean, they can't have left the coat-hooks off.

HARCOURT: These details can be overlooked in moments of enthusiasm. They left the staircase out in my house.

DAVID (finally): Of all the extraordinary things to omit. Coat-hooks. One does despair, really.

(Goes to the phone to dial.)

JOYCE: My goodness, yes.

AMY: It'll be very beautiful to look at. Perhaps we should name it after you, David.

JOYCE (DAVID speaks on phone during speech): Oh yes, do let's. And when it's finished we can get on with the new assembly block.

HARCOURT: Your arena stage, Miss Pinnington.

JOYCE: Yes, Mr Harcourt.

HARCOURT: The Pinnington block.

(DAVID is on the phone.)

DAVID: Maddening. The idiots can't find their copy of the plan. How on earth some people are so badly organised – Hello? Yes, that's the number. Now, perhaps you can see the coat-hooks.

(A knock and the SCHOOL SECRETARY appears.)

SECRETARY: Oh. I didn't realise you were in conference, Headmaster.

DAVID: Just see if you can find any coat-hooks here.

SECRETARY: Letters for signature.

(She puts them down and peers at the plans.)

JOYCE: At least they put in the laboratories.

DAVID: Laboratories are no use without coat-hooks. It's such a lovely day, too.

HARCOURT (to AMY about sherry): Not for her.

DAVID (into phone): What? Exactly, there aren't any. Of course they need them.

(Mildly firm):

If I say they need coat-hooks, they need coat-hooks. Well, ring back as soon as you know.

(He puts the phone down.)

Clearly they've forgotten all about them. Now, has everyone got sherry?

(The SECRETARY hasn't.)

AMY: Are there five of us?.

DAVID: One, two, three, four, five, yes.

(He takes a glass for himself, the SECRETARY and JOYCE. HARCOURT has to pour another for himself.)

Well, to the science labs.

ALL: Hear, hear, well done, yes.

DAVID: Long may they last.

AMY: Surely they'll be out   ten years.

DAVID: What? Why?

AMY: Progress, David.

DAVID: Oh yes. Yes, of course. Progress.

(He laughs, partly with discomfort, partly with good humour.)

JOY: The block may be a flexible structure, built to absorb new modular units.

DAVID: Let's have a look.

(All close round the plan except SECRETARY who moves clear.)

SECRETARY: I don't know, Dr Cornwallis, if it's any use, but there's a covered way leading to the new block from the swimming pool exit at the rear of this one.

DAVID: What? Where?

HARCOURT: Oh, yes.

AMY: Where?

HARCOURT: There.

JOYCE: Oh!

(They stare at it.)

DAVID (reaches for the phone): Excuse me.

SECRETARY: It was just a suggestion.

DAVID (dialling): Quite right. It answers everything.
No need for coat-hooks.

SECRETARY: I know you teachers have so much on your
minds that you sometimes don't see the obvious thing.

(HARCOURT, AMY, JOYCE and DAVID stare at her.)

DAVID (suddenly into the phone): Hullo? David Cornwallis
here.I rang just now about those...Yes. No, well
you're quite right we don't need any. There appears
to be a covered way,

(To the others):

Where is it?

(They point.)

By the metal workshop. Yes. You see it? No, we
didn't realise, either, till my secretary pointed it out.
Yes, very foolish. Thank you.

(Replaces receiver, stares at SECRETARY for a
minute.)

Would you like to say how long the new buildings will
keep pace with scientific advance?

SECRETARY: Oh, I was never any good at science.

DAVID: Hasn't it been any use to you?

SECRETARY: English was always my favourite, Mr
Harcourt, though French is coming in now we have
holidays abroad.

DAVID: Hasn't science been any use to you at all?

SECRETARY: Nor Latin.

DAVID: Science and Latin? I wonder if school is useless.

SECRETARY (shocked): Oh no.

DAVID: Knowledge - perhaps it's all useless.

SECRETARY (shocked): Of course not.

DAVID: You don't think so?

SECRETARY (surprised he doesn't know): It's education.

DAVID: I'd forgotten. Yes. Very important.

(The telephone rings. AMY answers it.)

AMY: Hullo? Yes, we've discovered it. Thank you. Goodbye.

(She replaces the receiver.)

The architect's office to tell us there's a covered way.

(An awkward silence, then):

SECRETARY: Well, I must get back to work. No free periods for secretaries, you know.

(She laughs.)

What a busy life!

(She goes.)

DAVID: What fools we were to miss it. It's obvious when you know where it is.

AMY: I love covered ways.

JOYCE: How Freudian.

HARCOURT: Oh, Lord.

JOYCE: Well, isn't it?

HARCOURT: I'm happy to say I've no idea.

DAVID (bursting out): It's not being able to trust people that's so appalling. I tell you, it makes life unlivable. These architects are so incompetent it drives one to the end of one's tether.

JOYCE: Yes.

DAVID: Nobody can tell if there's a covered way or not unless they see it on the plan, but do they write it in clearly?

JOYCE: No.

DAVID: And we end up doing the architect's job for him.

DAVID: Shut up! (Surprised.) I'm so sorry, Joyce. I don't know what came over me.

JOYCE: I – I didn't mean –

DAVID: No, no, I know that.

JOYCE: I'm awfully sorry.

DAVID: That's quite all right.

JOYCE: I mean –

AMY: Joyce! For heaven's sake!

JOYCE: But I so agree with Dr Cornwallis. It's so
frustrating when people don't do what you want them
to do. I mean what they're supposed to do.

DAVID: I've no doubt we shall manage in spite of their
foolishness. Eh, John?

HARCOURT: I'm sure it'll go very nicely, Headmaster.
However, I must go and try to coax some O level passes
out of 5C. Not inspiring.

JOYCE: I always find the C streams great fun.

HARCOURT: I'm not a bit surprised, and when I've had
the benefit of experience such as yours I shall doubt-
less come to the same remarkable conclusion. For you,
Paradise may be a fair field full of such groups through
which the Rousseau–esque mind can romp in glory. For
me, 5C are the dregs. I hope your science block is a
great success, Headmaster, and I'll see you later,
Mrs Selkirk, to discuss the evidently insignificant
matter of continued stealing.

(He goes out. JOYCE tries not to cry.)

JOYCE: I didn't mean to upset him.

DAVID: What was that about stealing?

AMY: There's a lot of stealing in the school.

DAVID: Oh, God! People are so petty.

AMY: John Harcourt's dealing with it. And I believe Reg,
though he's overworked, he says.

DAVID: (suddenly angry): Oh, Reg!

(Bangs the desk.)

These plans have been designed to pull this school
further forward than any other school in the county.
They constitute a vision of the future. Amy, there is

a vision of the future?

AMY: Yes, David, I'm sure there is.

JOYCE: Of course there is! How can you say there isn't?

DAVID: She hasn't.

JOYCE: But it's awful the way some people are so slack and unimaginative.

DAVID: She's not unimaginative.

AMY: Thank you.

DAVID: I appointed her.

JOYCE: Yes, of course. I'm so sorry.

DAVID: She's very enthusiastic about my plans, aren't you, Amy?

AMY: Yes, they're very pretty. I'll see you later, David.

JOYCE (To AMY): Why am I so annoying?

AMY (vague): Perhaps it's the way you were brought up.

(Sympathetic):

I'm so sorry.

DAVID (looking at his plans): They disapprove of you as much as they disapprove of me, don't they?

JOYCE (trying not to cry, nods):

DAVID: It would help if you weren't in love with me.

(JOYCE is stunned.)

DAVID: What I mean is, it would help me.

JOYCE: Am I in love with you?

DAVID: You've been miserable about it for years.

JOYCE: I suppose so.

DAVID: Yes. Having got it clear, will you be able to do something about it?

JOYCE: I don't think so.

DAVID: Oh, dear.

JOYCE: I'll try, of course, but I can't be sure that I'll be able to pull it off.

DAVID: That's unlike you.

JOYCE: I know. I feel rather feeble.

DAVID: It is annoying that the one thing I want you to do is the one thing you can't do. I don't love you in the least.

JOYCE: No. I've always known that, anyway.

DAVID: There is one thing I'd like you to promise me not to do.

JOYCE: Hand in my resignation?

DAVID: Good girl! Did they call you Pinners at school?

JOYCE (nearly crying): Yes.

DAVID (cheerily): Well, chin up, Pinners. You can jolly well do it if you try.

JOYCE (in tears at last): Why does everyone know everything about me?

(Bell rings.)

SCENE FOUR

A corridor. AMY crosses at the same time as JANET and SIMPSON who are holding hands. She looks surprised at SIMPSON's record player lid. SIMPSON and JANET go off. JOE appears.

JOE: Young love. I always think it looks very pretty.

AMY: Aren't you teaching?

JOE: There's been a breakdown among the musical instruments.

AMY (baffled): Oh. Well, I wouldn't wait here, if I were you.

(She indicates REG's room where we can see REG and RAYMOND with their heads together.)

JOE: Can't you feel the awful calm seeping out? They're fissile material, those two. If something thrilling happened in their lives their limbs would fly off in all directions with a great bang.

(He approaches the door.)

AMY: They?

JOE: There's always two in there, hatching.

(Shouting):

The king is dead, long live the king!

(He leaves. REG and RAYMOND look at each other. RAYMOND comes to the door and looks out.)

AMY (as she leaves): Good morning, Raymond. Teaching 4A again, I see.

(RAYMOND closes the door and goes back to the desk.)

RAYMOND: The Senior Mistress.

RAYMOND: It didn't sound like the Senior Mistress.

RAYMOND: The only person there was the Senior Mistress.

REG (quietly, darkly): Sometimes I feel this room is in the eye of a hurricane.

(They go back to looking at lists, heads bent together.)

SCENE FIVE

The HEADMASTER's office. The SMALL BOY is standing at the open door, BOY coughs.

DAVID: Mm?

SMALL BOY: I've been sent to you by Mr Macalpine, sir.

DAVID: He's teaching at last, is he?

SMALL BOY: Oh!

DAVID: What?

SMALL BOY: That's why I'm here.

DAVID: Why?

SMALL BOY: Because that's what I said. To Mr Macalpine. You're teaching at last.

DAVID: That was cheeky.

SMALL BOY: Yes, sir.

DAVID: There are actions, times and places which when they coincide are right, and when they don't coincide are wrong. Unhappily when you referred to Mr Macalpine's lateness the time and place were wrong, whereas when I referred to Mr Macalpine's lateness the time and the place were right. You, therefore, must be punished, and I need not be.

SMALL BOY: Yes, sir.

DAVID: Now, if you can get the answer right to this question, I'll let you off any further punishment. What is missing from this plan?

SMALL BOY: Nothing, sir.

DAVID (smiling): Now what would you say if I said to you, 'Yes, something is missing. Coat-hooks is missing'. What would you reply then?

SMALL BOY: Wouldn't this covered way obviate the need for coat-hooks, sir?

DAVID: How did you know it was a covered way?

SMALL BOY: It says so.

DAVID: Where?

SMALL BOY: There, sir, in print.

DAVID: Have you just written that there?

SMALL BOY: No, sir.

DAVID: It wasn't there before, was it?

SMALL BOY: Before what, sir?

DAVID: Perhaps it was and none of us noticed it.

SMALL BOY: Yes, sir.

DAVID (after a pause): Do you believe in God?

SMALL BOY: Believe in Him, sir?

DAVID: The great planner?

SMALL BOY: Yes, sir.

DAVID: Quite right. This is an auspicious beginning

to your career.

SMALL BOY: I'm in my second year, sir.

DAVID: We must always have plans, even in the second year.

SMALL BOY: Yes, sir.

DAVID: The boardrooms of the world are filled with men who learnt to plan before they learnt anything else, and today, in this study, we've had a glimpse into one of tomorrow's boardrooms.

SMALL BOY: Yes, sir.

DAVID: D'you understand?

SMALL BOY: No, sir.

DAVID: You will in time. Now off you go. And feel free to call whenever you have a problem.

SMALL BOY: Yes, sir. Goodbye, sir.

DAVID (peering at his plans): Goodbye.

(The SMALL BOY goes.)

DAVID: How could I have missed it? How could I have missed it!

(Angry):

Oh, God, give me strength!

SCENE SIX

A corridor.

JOE: Joyce!

JOYCE: I've really nothing I can possibly say to you, Joe. I mean, you know very well all there is to know about me, so I might as well just run away and die. Have you got a tambourine?

JOE: You aren't transparent. I don't know anything about you at all.

JOYCE: Really? Have you got a tambourine?

JOE: What would you do if something went wrong that couldn't be put right? Something that brought the school to a sudden halt?

JOYCE: How thrilling!

JOE: Could you play the piano in assembly for example.

JOYCE: Oh, Joe I'd love to! Are you joking?

JOE: Joking? If it's necessary for you to play in assembly I'll try to get a note to you. You'll need a piece of paper to say it's all right. Yes, I'll get you a tambourine.

(He goes.)

JOYCE: Joe – is something worrying you?

(SIMPSON approaches and passes, holding the lid. JOYCE looks surprised.)

Simpson!

(She leaves. Bell rings.)

SCENE SEVEN

The scene is the staff common room which is on the ground floor and has large glass doors opening out on to the grass outside where SHEILA is lying in shorts.

In the staff room are MIKE, AMY and HARRY CLOPTON who wears a white overall coat.

HARRY: Bloody Headmaster says to me, 'Harry,' he says, 'something'll have to be done about the advanced physics lab.' 'Yes,' I says, 'it'll have to be built.' 'Ah,' he says, 'but the designs are limited. It needs a cinema screen and a wide angled lens,

MIKE: Marvellous. Film society and all that.

HARRY: 'No bloody fear,' I said. 'If you want a cinema screen,' I said, 'You can raise the money at a PTA fete,' I said, 'but the taxpayer isn't going to finance a bloody Odeon in my labs.'

MIKE: Pity.

(MIKE is marking books throughout this scene.)

HARRY: The practical philistine always wins, Mac-alpine. You'd better get used to it.

MIKE: I've got used to enough. I don't intend to get used to any more.

AMY (at notice board): Since Reg Parsons signs his notices D H M I think I'll sign mine S M. Not having a room of my own makes me hard to define.

HARRY: This is my first free period in three weeks and the first time I've been in this staff room all term. How's that for hard work?

MIKE: Really in touch with the way your colleagues think.

HARRY: I'm here to do a job. I think I can say I do it with a clearer conscience than some.

AMY: What job are you here to do, Harry?

HARRY: I'm not being drawn into anything abstruse. I work, and I know what I mean by work. And I might as well admit I'm a prey to raging desire for the P E department.

(He gazes through the window at her.)

AMY: Aren't you happy, Harry?

HARRY: Happy? Yes. Raging desire is a very happy thing, Amy. However,

(Looking towards MIKE):

Sheila's booked by the imaginative languages assistant.

MIKE: I'm married.

HARRY: She told me she thought you were a fascist.

AMY: Sheila's a silly girl.

HARRY: She does her job.

AMY (cross): We all do our jobs, Harry.

HARRY: Do we. All right.

(New subject.)

What about Janet What's-Her-Name, goes round with

Simpson?

AMY: She's very nice. She's unintelligent.

MIKE: She's beautiful.

HARRY: She wants to be a teacher. She comes to me for extra tuition.

MIKE: She comes to us all for extra tuition.

AMY: Year after year someone wants to be cleverer than they are.

MIKE: We aren't very clever in this profession. She could do it pretty well. The lower streams. She wants to do it, Amy.

HARRY: Wanting isn't enough. Even we philistines know that.

AMY: It's always the same.

MIKE: Don't you hate this job? Every day it runs into an agony of some kind which it's powerless to help. It's the most powerless job in the world.

AMY: I enjoy life even when it's unsatisfactory. None of my daily failures makes me despair.

HARRY: People are what they are. You can't alter them, and Janet is stupid.

MIKE: That's an idle attitude.

HARRY: Idle? Me?

AMY: Yes.

(Consulting watch):

John Harcourt should be here for his mid-lesson break.

HARRY: There's idleness, if you like. Mathballs Harcourt.

MIKE: It's torture to think of him blocking the way to their imaginations. It's clause analysis every time they show signs of enjoyment.

(HARCOURT comes in.)

HARRY: Ah! Extension of the verb Harcourt. Harcourt the participial. They call you Mathballs, don't they John?

(HARCOURT has gone straight to the board.)

MIKE: There are times when you're so lazy I wonder if you feel ashamed. I don't suppose you do.

HARCOURT: I don't think so, no.

MIKE: We're supposed to do a job in this society and some of us think it's an important one.

HARCOURT: I'm very glad to hear it. Truisms aren't necessarily invalid.

MIKE: Harcourt!

HARCOURT (still at notices): Yes?

MIKE: What is your class doing?

HARCOURT: Work. Was your's doing work at half-past-nine?

HARRY: You're paid to confront your classes. You don't bloody do it. That makes you a thief, in my opinion.

HARCOURT: Come, Harry, there are notices to read.

HARRY: There's break.

HARCOURT: I've a department to run.

HARRY: So've I.

HARCOURT: I find that takes all my time.

HARRY: Rubbish.

HARCOURT: And then there are disturbances, like stealing, or masters throwing record players out of windows. All time consuming. You saw it, I believe, Macalpine.

MIKE: He was frustrated. Ask him yourself.

HARCOURT: I have.

MIKE: I can't add anything.

HARCOURT: Time you see, it all goes running by.

MIKE: You could fulfil your duty to your classes by exposing them to your imagination even so. You don't do that. You don't begin to do it. You're useless.

HARCOURT: Oh, Amy, Janet Thingummy.

AMY: You give her extra tuition.

HARCOURT: She wants to be a teacher.

MIKE: She's a pretty girl. You're still an active man. The amount of work you do here doesn't absorb all the energy available.

HARCOURT (tartly): I sometimes wonder if you've ever noticed there are boys in this school.

MIKE: You've noticed the boys, Harcourt?

HARCOURT (cross): I'm a married man.

(Weak smile.)

I don't mean to sound puritanical but sometimes the conversation in here does seem rather obvious.

MIKE: I'm a married man and I have children. I'd like to think of them enjoying English when they come to school eventually.

HARCOURT: I'd naturally forgotten you were married. Well, Janet certainly won't make a teacher. She hasn't got what it takes.

(He goes out.)

MIKE (shouting): How do you know!

HARRY: This is my free period and I intend to enjoy it.

(He goes out and lies down beside SHEILA.)

AMY: The walls of this school are some of the most beautiful I've ever seen. I was raised in the Midlands. I hated English because the exercise books were a dirty brown, and I took up French because of the smell of coffee. I'd never smelt coffee in my life, but I had an idea about it. Later on, when I smelt it in France after the war it was exactly as I thought it would be. That's why I'm Head of Languages, and that's why I enjoy teaching them.

MIKE: I don't enjoy teaching anything. I don't enjoy any of the daily features of my life. I'm overwhelmed.

AMY: I think it must be my nature. When I look at myself in the mirror I have no illusions. My nose is undistinguished and I'm getting thick about the middle. But when I see this building in the sunshine like this, I feel I'm slim and have a flat tummy and a pretty face. All the compressed little stodginesses of my

character are teased away; and I want to run naked
in the sun and have faint, pleasant sensations without
involvement.

MIKE (at work correcting): Le maison. Dear God, le
maison!

(They sit in silence, AMY doing nothing, MIKE
marking.)

SCENE EIGHT

The HEADMASTER's office. DAVID faces JANET.

DAVID: You're Janet Thingumebob.

JANET: Yes, sir.

DAVID: I've heard of you.

JANET: I was afraid so.

DAVID: You're Simpson's girl friend.

JANET: There's nothing exclusive about it.

(They laugh.)

And you're the Headmaster.

DAVID: Ah, yes, Janet. The Headmaster.

JANET: I've come to see you about my career.

DAVID: Yes.

(He looks out of his window downwards.)

Why is Simpson carrying the lid of a record player?

JANET: Mr Johnson gave it him.

DAVID: Gave it to him?

JANET: Please, sir, my career.

DAVID: You're a nice girl, Janet. Are you trying to
cover something up for your boy friend?

JANET: No, sir.

DAVID: Is he part of your career? One of your plans?

JANET: I don't think so.

DAVID: The fluid approach of course is the correct one. But sometime you'll have to decide, Janet, and make up your mind about something. Look at these.

(A great mass of plans.)

JANET (looking at them): They're very pretty.

DAVID (slowly): What strikes you as the most useful thing about the new science block?

JANET: There's no disposal bins for the girl's toilets.

DAVID: No what?

JANET: Nothing.

DAVID: Disposal bins? They aren't chemical toilets, you know.

JANET: I shouldn't have mentioned it. Oh, look – a covered way to the main building.

DAVID: There's one of those revolving towels, too, not paper ones. See, there's the towel. What's that dispenser for, then?

(He reaches for the phone.)

I'd better get on to someone.

(He begins to dial.)

JANET (putting her hand on the receiver): No.

DAVID: Janet, I am the Headmaster.

JANET: Those things are intimate.

DAVID (putting down the receiver): Oh.

JANET: Mrs Selkirk'll see to it later.

DAVID: Oh.

JANET: That covered way is very good.

DAVID: Yes.

JANET: It'll be lovely doing science over there. I want to be a teacher, sir.

DAVID: I'm afraid I still don't understand, even now. Do we have these things already in the school?

JANET: Yes.

DAVID: I expect if I were married I'd know what we
were talking about.

JANET: It's not all that important. It's getting into
training college that's going to be difficult.

(The bell rings.)

DAVID: That's break. You'll have to go, I suppose.

JANET: I came to talk about my career, Dr Cornwallis.

DAVID: Yes. Well, we'll need time to discuss that.
Come back when you're not so busy.

JANET: Thank you sir.

DAVID: Not at all. I'm always here to talk to.

(JANET goes.)

I don't know. Disposal bins...

(He shakes his head.)

SCENE NINE

The common room, at coffee time. If possible there should
be many extras present besides the main characters.

REG, RAYMOND, HARCOURT coffee cups in hand.

REG: Harcourt, they've got to wear them. My authority
will have been called in question if a fool like Macalpine gets away with clothes like his any more. I feel
affronted every time I see him.

RAYMOND: A vision led me into this profession, Harcourt, and clothed me in the weeds of learning. I
often imagined myself as a master or a provost or
some fine figure strolling on a lawn –

REG: Are you insulting me?

RAYMOND: What?

REG: You know I went to Birmingham.

HARCOURT: And I to Leeds.

RAYMOND: My true home is the Gothic, the pale perpendicular of Kings. I wonder why I left it.

REG: You got a bad degree.

RAYMOND: Yes.

REG: In fact you nearly failed.

RAYMOND: I've not been lucky.

REG: You were lucky to come here.

(MIKE, HARRY, SHEILA.)

MIKE: I'd like a teaching machine as well, then I could sit on the grass with Sheila.

SHEILA (to MIKE): You're marvellously fascist.

HARRY: Christ.

SHEILA: Too many men are merely pretty.

(JOE and MIKE.)

JOE: Have you ever seen Reg Parsons crying over his wife's death?

MIKE: She's still alive.

JOE: But he cries over her death quite often. It's very moving.

(AMY and RAYMOND.)

AMY: And they've all gone to the forest of Dean, just like that.

RAYMOND: Regular scrutiny of the board would keep you up to date.

AMY: A personal note would've been courteous.

RAYMOND: Time doesn't always allow.

HARRY: Not that it's any of his business.

RAYMOND: Pardon?

HARRY: The Deputy Headmaster should attend to that.

(JOE and JOYCE.)

JOYCE: That was an interesting conversation we had earlier.

JOE: I promise you the tambourine.

JOYCE: And what was Simpson doing with a record player lid?

JOE: It isn't possible to say, really.

(AMY, MIKE, HARRY.)

AMY: Shall I speak to Janet?

HARRY: She's got to know her chances.

MIKE: You can't decide a thing like that over coffee.

HARRY: Facts are facts.

MIKE: We don't exactly know what they are.

HARRY: I do. She's stupid.

MIKE: It's her future, Harry.

JOE (to everyone): Can I have a word with you, please?

(REG, RAYMOND, HARCOURT.)

REG: He threw a record player out of his room this morning. It adds up, you know.

JOE: I'm afraid there's been some more stealing. This time a girl in my class, Gertrude Hum.

(Amusement.)

She's had her bicycle stolen.

(Great amusement.)

This morning apparently. If any of you see Gertrude Hum's bicycle will you let me know?

(REG, RAYMOND, HARCOURT.)

RAYMOND: The simple fact is he doesn't wear a gown. That's why Gertrude Hum lost her bicycle.

HARCOURT: Can we talk about stealing, Deputy Head-master?

REG: Of course, we must be fair. If we aren't fair, we shall make a mistake.

HARCOURT: This stealing –

RAYMOND: We've been fair too long. By throwing a record player out of his window Joe Johnson has brought the good name of this school into disgrace and been dis-loyal to his colleagues.

REG: Are you quoting me?

RAYMOND (surprised): No.

REG: Go on, then.

RAYMOND: Haven't I said enough?

REG: For me you have.

HARCOURT: If you could spare a minute.

JOE (approaching REG): You don't look very well, this morning, Mr Parsons.

(By now the staff have all gone outside with their cups of coffee. If they can be seen they are admiring the gymnastic feats of SHEILA who is showing off to MIKE. HARCOURT, REG and RAYMOND gaze at JOE in silence.)

REG (eventually): Do I not?

JOE: You wear too many clothes. Look at Sheila. She's got the right idea.

(He smiles enigmatically.)

REG: We are built rather differently.

(RAYMOND laughs sycophantically. REG smiles with quiet self satisfaction, and they sail out followed by the fussing HARCOURT. At this moment the SECRETARY appears and finds she is caught in JOE's stare.)

SECRETARY(nervously): Why aren't you outside?

JOE: I was waiting for you.

(Singing the slow movement from Mozart's clarinet concerto he takes her in his arms and begins to dance with great languor. She is surprised.)

CURTAIN

Act Two

SCENE ONE

The HEADMASTER's office.

DAVID is practising swings with a cane. He talks to himself as he does so.

DAVID: Is the boy guilty or not? No answer, you see. Yes, says the evidence. No, says the boy.

(He stops practising, and looks up.)

And You, You say nothing at all. Probably because You aren't there. So I can't blame You. Nevertheless, within minutes I must decide whether to thrash him or let him go. I must even try –

(There is a knock at the door.)

Come in! – to decide –

(The SECRETARY comes in with letters.)

if there's any virtue of any kind in punishment anyway.

SECRETARY: Oh, yes.

DAVID: I doubt it. No-one ever stops being bad.

(He comes to the desk to sign things.)

SECRETARY: Punishment's obvious, isn't it?

DAVID: I wish I knew.

SECRETARY: It is to me.

DAVID: To you so many things are obvious you must be Tiresias come to life. What an excellent husband you must make for some poor man.

(The SECRETARY laughs.)

I didn't mean to be offensive.

SECRETARY: You weren't.

DAVID: What a relief.

SECRETARY: You need a holiday, don't you?

(She takes the signed letters. He goes on talking as if

she were still there.)

DAVID: I doubt if that's enough. You're an excellent secretary, though of course you're paid to be. We're all paid for something. I'm paid to educate, to lead people into the light –

(There is a knock. SIMPSON enters with the lid.)

Come in – which is far from easy. I? Lead?

(DAVID looks at SIMPSON):

Have you ever led anyone?

SIMPSON: No, sir.

DAVID: Not even across a road?

SIMPSON: Oh yes, sir. Old ladies.

DAVID: How did you feel?

SIMPSON: Good.

DAVID: I have to know, Simpson, if you stole Gertrude Hum's bicycle as Mr Harcourt seems to think you did. I want you to say, 'Yes, I stole Gertrude Hum's bicycle. Mr Harcourt is quite right.'

(SIMPSON says nothing.)

You see! You don't do it. And I am paid to make a decision on so little evidence.

SIMPSON: Sir.

DAVID: I'm paid also to lead the youth of England into the riches – the riches – of – of –

SIMPSON (pat): Man's unconquerable mind.

DAVID: And to broaden their experience, and ensure that every boy – and every girl – is –

SIMPSON: Stretched to his or her fullest capacity and matched to...

SIMPSON and DAVID: his or her particlar skill.

DAVID: And I don't. I grope blindly.

SIMPSON: Sir.

DAVID: I grope forward, I hope.

SIMPSON: Sir.

DAVID: But sometimes backwards, too.

SIMPSON: Sir. Should you be telling me all this?

DAVID: I'm not telling you. You're overhearing it.

SIMPSON: It never occurs to us that you don't know exactly what you're doing.

DAVID: I often know what I'm doing and when I don't I usually cover up pretty well. This is a rather special occasion.

(He offers cigarettes.)

Do you smoke?

SIMPSON: Yes, sir.

DAVID: Well, you shouldn't! There, whether I like it or not, I've been biased against you. Where is the scientific method?

SIMPSON: Would you like to sit down, sir?

DAVID: No, thank you. I would find it painfully re-stricting.

SIMPSON: D'you mind if I do?

DAVID: No.

(SIMPSON sits.)

What a remarkable boy to be able to sit at such a moment, clutching, I see, the only concrete evidence we have.

SIMPSON: Yes, sir.

DAVID: How did you get it?

SIMPSON: All you need to know is that I didn't steal it, sir.

DAVID: I'd be quite happy to believe you, Simpson, but the circumstances surrounding that lid are somewhat peculiar, and there is an epidemic of stealing.

SIMPSON: Yes, sir.

DAVID: You know, I suppose, Mr Macalpine's wild story that Mr Johnson made the lid a kind of philosophical presentation to you.

SIMPSON: Yes, sir.

DAVID: What do you say?

SIMPSON: Nothing.

DAVID: That's what Mr Johnson says too. This is not
the sort of situation a university degree prepares
you for.

SIMPSON: I suppose not, sir.

DAVID: I think I'd better have that lid.

SIMPSON: Could you be more precise.

DAVID: Put the lid on the desk, will you
Simpson.

SIMPSON: No, sir.

DAVID: Why not?

SIMPSON: I have to keep it.

DAVID: Have to keep it?

SIMPSON: It seems correct to me, in this situation, that
I should keep it.

DAVID: Why?

SIMPSON: It's a conclusion I've arrived at instinctively.

DAVID: But it's not yours. Give it back!

SIMPSON: I can't, sir! Let's talk about something else.

DAVID: We can't talk about anything else. You've come
here especially to talk about this, and that's the
whole point of the interview.

SIMPSON: I didn't steal Gertrude Hum's bicycle, or any
of the other things Mr Harcourt thinks he's pinned on
me. I swear I didn't.

DAVID: I never thought you did.

SIMPSON: Then let me keep the lid.

DAVID: How can I? It's been paid for by the county. How
can I let it go when I've been paid for by the county,
too, specifically to stop you taking it.

SIMPSON: You're in a dilemma.

DAVID: Oh, yes. I'm the superior kind of creature who

can get into dilemmas, the sort who never makes the grade. I have no blind duty, no blind instinct.

SIMPSON: And you can't let the whole thing go.

DAVID (slowly): No, not unless there's been some considerable mistake. Some – massive – mistake.

SIMPSON: Sir?

DAVID: This instituion – school – requires of its Headmaster that he prevents his pupils possessing county property like the lids of record players. Now suppose the institution ought never to have been invented? Suppose schools are the wrong thing?

SIMSPSON: Sir?

DAVID: Let me illustrate.

Suppose a farmer has some cows and he feeds them up to get meat from them. Because he doesn't milk them, they die in agony. He notices they are in less pain lying down than standing so the next lot of cows he has he chains to the floor. They die, so thinking the trouble must be in the legs themselves, he cuts the legs off the third lot of cows he has. Then he tries breeding cows without legs, thinking that's the answer. All the time, you see, misunderstanding the whole point about cows. Suppose we have made a huge misunderstanding about men and women and knowledge, and schools are altogether the wrong thing?

SIMPSON: Yes. I see. That would be bad for you.

DAVID: Exactly. For me.

SIMPSON: Actually, you know what you're going to do.

DAVID: The wrong thing.

SIMPSON: One doesn't see how you can avoid it. The pattern seems complete.

DAVID: It seems overriding. In science it would be overriding.

SIMPSON: And you feel a strong compulsion to beat me, don't you?

DAVID: Now I have the cane, yes.

SIMPSON: And now you have the cane I feel a strong compulsion to submit, I'm innocent, though, and you can't have the lid.

DAVID: Please.

SIMPSON: No.

DAVID: Bend over, then.

SIMPSON: Any particular place?

DAVID: Over this chair. Let me show you the position I like best.

(He does so.)

SIMPSON: Like?

DAVID: Like isn't the word, but this position helps me to execute my duty better than any other. Now get down.

(SIMPSON puts the lid on the chair and bends down.)

SIMPSON: I shan't bump my head on anything when I jump, shall I?

DAVID: No.

SIMPSON: Right.

DAVID: Here we go, then.

(He struggles to lift the cane and fails.)

I'm afraid I can't lift the cane up.

SIMPSON: Can I do it for you?

DAVID: Yes. I don't suppose we can excuse ourselves from the obvious solution.

(SIMPSON gives it to him.)

Thank you.

(SIMPSON goes back. DAVID struggles to bring the cane down. Bell goes. Stops.)

Now, I'm afraid I can't bring it down.

SIMPSON (getting up): Is there any way out of that?

DAVID: I don't think there is.

SIMPSON: You aren't cheating?

DAVID: I've never cheated in my life! Sit down.

SIMPSON (releasing DAVID from his strange position): I'd rather not. I'd rather go.

DAVID (assuming authority): Very well, Simpson, I'll look into this matter more closely. In the meantime, I think I'd better look after that.

(He holds out his hand still holding the cane in the other.)

SIMPSON (handing over the lid): It isn't quite right.

DAVID: It's the best I can do.

(Each has a hand on it.)

I am the Headmaster, Simpson, whether we like it or not. I must have this lid.

(SIMPSON lets go.)

No. Take it back.

SIMPSON: You've got it.

DAVID: I don't want it.

SIMPSON: I'm sorry, sir.

DAVID: I don't want it, Simpson! Take it back!

SIMPSON: No, sir. I can't.

DAVID: Simpson!

SIMPSON: I'll go now, sir, if I may.

DAVID: Very well, Simpson.

(SIMPSON goes.)

Always the wrong thing. Always the wrong bloody thing!

(He sits unhappily at his desk.)

SCENE TWO

REG's office. REG and RAYMOND go into it.

REG: I'd like to be progressive. Progressives can afford to breathe more easily than I can, who, gifted with a certain modicum of vision, have to fight to reconcile so much. I never found myself in the vanguard, as they say, even as a student, and yet I wasn't a reactionary, Raymond, am not a reactionary I may add. But this desk, these notice boards - this job is not one I can trust to wild ideas, Raymond. I am Deputy Headmaster

(He begins looking through the drawers.)

and although there are so many things - so many things - I am the Deputy - and both sides -

(He slams the drawers shut.)

The stationery department should understand that drawing pins are vital to the good running of the school. Nobody has pins and there's developed an uneasy sense that everyone is taking other people's pins, until I'm driven to believe that somebody, perhaps no lesser person than the Senior Mistress herself, has been into this room, up to this desk, and rifled through these drawers. There are no pins! Notices litter my desk. The boards are cluttered even though I rearrange them frequently, and no one knows how vitally important clear notice boards become when administration has to be checked, and rechecked, and double checked, and treble checked. Progressives never think in terms like that. They never think. And when we try to show in simple reasonable terms that gowns are part of a teacher's basic equipment, what will be said? A lot of high falutin' verbiage about ideals. Well, no one has higher ideals than me, a place for everything and everything in its place, but take Macalpine. We shall have the New Statesman thrown up at us before we know where we are.

RAYMOND: In education, I'm conservative.

REG: Let's not bring politics into it, Raymond. One mustn't you see, - how shall I put it? - verbalise too much. My job is one for which I feel uniquely fitted, I would say. It is the post of one who watches over all with that sane outlook, well-washed, clearly lit, that the best of our liberal forbears cherished in us all. Conserve what is right, adapt what is wrong, evolution not revolution, never be the first and never be the last.

RAYMOND: A good middle of the roader.

REG: What?

RAYMOND: A good –

REG (interrupting): There you go, you see, Raymond verbalising. Catchpenny phrases that smack of glossy Sunday journalism.

RAYMOND: What I meant was –

REG: What you said was middle of the roader. I like to think I've more in me than that. A sheep is a middle of the roader.

RAYMOND: Yes.

REG: Then if you didn't mean that I was a sheep, which I take it you did not, what did you mean?

RAYMOND: I think I meant that you were a person who believed in evolution, not revolution.

REG: I didn't say I believed that. I said it characterised the outlook of our best liberal forbears.

RAYMOND: I think I take the point you're trying to make.

REG: Trying to make?

RAYMOND: Making, then.

REG: What condescension!

RAYMOND: What?

REG: You must learn to watch your words, young man.

RAYMOND: I think I'm capable of understanding words, Deputy Headmaster.

REG: Oh! Really!

RAYMOND: What d'you mean?

REG: You don't get things done by shattering the school's continuum, destroying the school's balance, or anarchy of that sort.

RAYMOND: I'm not trying to. I want us to get our gowns.

REG: I've told you once, Raymond, and I'll tell you again, that is a matter for common room to decide in camera.

RAYMOND: Then what are we discussing?

REG: Ways and means.

RAYMOND: For what?

REG: Well, there you are, then, there you are, that's what we're discussing.

(There is a silence in which RAY glances surreptitiously at his watch.)

RAYMOND: Ah – um – perhaps in the meantime, as it were, it might be advisable for me to slip back to my class, Deputy Headmaster.

(He gets up.)

REG: What?

RAYMOND: Pardon?

REG: You're teaching?

RAYMOND: Yes.

REG: Now?

RAYMOND: In the library. The sixth.

REG: You've left them?

RAYMOND: They're working by themselves.

REG: Are you making a name for yourself in common room as a person who pursues an existence enjoyable for reasons other than the most laudable pleasures?

RAYMOND (after a second or two): Most certainly not.

REG: It would be an unpleasant but unavoidable duty to have to point out the scruples we expect of our colleagues if I suspected anyone, no matter whom of such a practice.

RAYMOND (trying to leave): Of course.

REG: If only one could trust you to do your jobs. If only one knew what every mind was thinking. If one had their habits of thought one could put in train the running of the school the way it ought to go. That's the way of achieving what is democratically best for everyone. One must have their minds, or else it is coercion. Do you understand, Raymond?

(Whether he does or not, RAYMOND nods.)

You'd better go, young man.

(He does. Unhappily he crosses the stage. He is bumped into by SIMPSON who apologises. RAYMOND merely shakes his head and goes slowly off. In the meantime

REG is taking down his notices and pinning them back
where they were before. SIMPSON goes into JOE's
classroom, looks round and eventually approaches the
cupboard. He throws it open. JOE is seated there on
a high stool.)

SCENE THREE

There is a light from a bare electric bulb. The shelves
are filled with stolen items and GERTRUDE HUM's
bicycle can be seen.

SIMPSON (amazed): I've suffered for all this stuff.

JOE: Did he beat you?

SIMPSON: He couldn't.

JOE: Good old David. He knew you were innocent.

SIMPSON: Oh, for goodness' sake. I tried to follow your
example and let that lid go where it had to. I didn't
try to force anything and in the end I was accused of all
this. It seems to me now is the moment for you to say
something.

JOE: It's very simple, Simpson, and you disappoint me
that you don't understand. You are innocent and I am
guilty. These two things are facts and we needn't
make a public spectacle about them. The truth will
simply appear, and that will be that.

SIMPSON: Mr Harcourt will be angry when he knows. All
those weeks of patient investigation.

JOE: I'm rather sorry about that. He doesn't deserve all
that trouble for nothing. One can't help feeling some
people are nice and others aren't. Just nice. Moth-
balls Harcourt is nice.

SIMPSON: I find this experience very disorientating.

JOE: You should. Most people will dismiss it as madness on
my part. They'll make odious comparisons between this
little room and my inner life, and that'll make them
very self-satisfied and difficult to bear.

SIMPSON: They'll want to know why you did it.

JOE: I suspect you do, too.

SIMPSON: I don't like to ask in case I appear foolish.

JOE: Well, it doesn't really matter, does it. I expect there's some reason. I might even be 'cured'. The fact is I did it. Now you have to tell someone what you've seen.

SIMPSON: Who?

JOE: So long as you tell the person you think will act immediately, so there's no dissipation, it doesn't matter,

SIMPSON: You mean go straight to the Head.

JOE: You must decide that, Simpson.

SIMPSON: Can't we forget it?

JOE: Of course not.

SIMPSON: I'd like to.

JOE: Because you find it squalid?

(No reply.)

Squalor's an unpleasant thing, and that's what I shall have to stand by. That's going to be the difficult part of living from now on. Will you please go and tell the Headmaster.

SIMPSON: I'll go, anyway.

(He leaves the classroom and doesn't shut the cupboard door.)

SCENE FOUR

A corridor. RAYMOND enters as if soliloquising. SIMPSON bumps into him.

SIMPSON: I'm sorry, sir, I didn't see you were there.

RAYMOND: Then look where you're going, boy.

SIMPSON: Yes, sir.

RAYMOND: Where are you going? This is a lesson.

SIMPSON: To see the Headmaster, sir.

(He leaves. RAYMOND coughs and rehearses a speech.)

RAYMOND: May I speak to you, Headmaster? Thank you.
I would like to speak not as a colleague, but as a man,
a man apart, apart, that is, from our profession,
viewing it with the eyes of a dispassionate observer.
It is a profession, Headmaster, of seers, <u>overseers</u>,
one might almost say, the guardians of the seeds of
knowledge, and guiders of the ways of men. Teachers,
Headmaster, are not ordinary mortals. They are –
Other. That is why I am a teacher, sir, because I am
Other, not as other men are but Other, as it were,
from other men. When, therefore, I consider your
establishment-

(HARCOURT enters unseen.)

I wonder how many other Other men there are here. Are
we really Other men, or merely other men?

(He pauses.)

Clarity, Raymond. A study of English should've taught
you that.

HARCOURT: The clarity of the timetable suggests you should
be in the library.

RAYMOND: I regard you, Harcourt, as a mental claudicator.

HARCOURT: Are you going to the library? To be Other
among the sixth?

RAYMOND: What are <u>you</u> doing?

HARCOURT: I'm looking for a gramophone record to illustrate the term Romantic. The library is that way.

(RAYMOND stamps off. HARCOURT goes into JOE's
room saying):

I sometimes wonder if this school is staffed entirely by
lunatics.

SCENE FIVE

JOE's classroom. HARCOURT stands amazed before the
store cupboard, where JOE still sits.

JOE: They might put me in prison.

HARCOURT: I beg your pardon.

JOE: Will you visit me?

HARCOURT (staring round): Good God.

JOE: Promise me, Harcourt? Visit me in prison and tell
    me what it's like out here? I'm afraid of prison, so
    will you help me with it?

HARCOURT: Am I right that these are the articles that
    have been stolen over the last year?

JOE: Yes.

HARCOURT: And that during my investigation you've
    known they were here?

JOE: Of course I've known they were here. I put them
    here. This is my store cupboard.

HARCOURT: Then you're the thief and Simpson isn't?

JOE: Yes, Harcourt.

HARCOURT: Well, I'll be hanged.

JOE: And when I go to prison, which I don't want to do...

HARCOURT: And you went on stealing them?

JOE: Please, Harcourt, will you visit me in prison?

HARCOURT: I really can't say, Joe. I suppose so, if
    there's no one else.

JOE: I went on stealing and now I've got to be discovered.

HARCOURT: What? Well, go and tell the Headmaster your-
    self.

JOE: Confession isn't the thing, John. Someone must
    reveal me in the middle of all this. It's the middle line.

HARCOURT: Well, bloody hell, that's all I can say. Bloody
    hell.

    (He stamps his feet.)

I'm sorry. You made me lose my temper.

JOE: It's enough to make you lose your temper having your friend turned into a thief before your eyes.

HARCOURT: There's some explanation, of course.

JOE: No, I'm just a thief. That is the bare classical fact. That is the thing I am and I'm not pretending to be otherwise.

HARCOURT: One can't just leave it there. There has to be some explanation.

JOE: Perhaps. It's the consequences that are important, however.

HARCOURT: I suppose those'll include your resignation.

JOE: Yes.

HARCOURT: Time will do the rest, Joe.

JOE: D'you think so?

HARCOURT: No. It was just something to say.

JOE: I may go to prison.

HARCOURT: That would be awful.

JOE: Will you visit me?

HARCOURT: Yes, Joe. Certainly. Of course I will. I'll bring the family.

JOE: Thank you.

HARCOURT: I suppose this is what they call fetichism, isn't it?

JOE: I don't know.

HARCOURT: Gertrude Hum's bicycle.

JOE: You'd better take your hand off the saddle before anyone comes in.

HARCOURT: What? Oh really!

(DAVID and SIMPSON come into the classroom.)

DAVID: Joe?

JOE: David?

DAVID: Is this true?

JOE: Obviously.

DAVID: I can't keep you on, you know.

JOE: I don't suppose you can recommend me, either.

DAVID: Harcourt? Are you connected with this?

HARCOURT: Only accidentally.

DAVID: And that bicycle is

(The other three together):

Gertrude Hum's.

DAVID: I owe you an apology, Simpson.

SIMPSON: That's all right, sir.

DAVID: No, no. You must accept it. My sincere apologies for accusing you of a crime you didn't commit.

SIMPSON: Thank you, sir.

HARCOURT: And my apologies, Simpson, for – for –

SIMPSON: Thank you, sir.

HARCOURT: Headmaster, you and I are very much at the centre of this thing just at the moment, being here, I mean, and with all the interested parties. Perhaps we could stop it unravelling and thereby spare ourselves the considerable loss of a friend.

DAVID: We can't stop it unravelling. This is a school. People don't come here to be robbed.

JOE: I've told you, John.

HARCOURT: I just thought – As you wish, Headmaster.

(The bell goes.)

SIMPSON: You must be properly discovered. Will you all stay still, please?

JOE: Of course.

(SIMPSON goes out.)

DAVID: Is he going to let your class in to see us?

JOE: Do you mind?

DAVID: It seems the least we can do.

JOE: Then shall we sing a little something, I being the

music master? Or shall we stay still and silent?

DAVID: Silence would have the greater symbolic significance, I think.

HARCOURT: I'd like to stand beside you, Joe.

JOE: Certainly, John.

DAVID: And I'll go on the other side.

(They take their places.)

DAVID: When you're ready, Simpson.

SIMPSON (off): Yes, sir.

HARCOURT: Are you going to be able to manage it, Joe?

JOE: Oh, yes. Quite easily.

HARCOURT: You, Headmaster?

DAVID: I think so.

HARCOURT: It's going to be an ordeal for me.

DAVID: Would you like us to stop it, Harcourt?

HARCOURT: Oh, no. It's the right thing.

DAVID: Stick it out, then.

HARCOURT: You too, Headmaster. It's maintaining the right face I'm finding difficult.

(The lights narrow on the figures. SIMPSON appears. The footsteps of pupils can be heard.)

SIMPSON: Right then, here they are. Well done, sir, well done all of you. Keep it up. Don't flinch.

(The sound of applause from the pupils.)

SCENE SIX

A corridor. AMY dithers there. MIKE joins her.

AMY: Mike! What is it about today?

MIKE: I don't know, but I wish it had been me who threw that record player away this morning. It would've cleared the air for me.

(DAVID pushes Gertrude Hum's bicycle across the stage.)

AMY: I wonder if that's Gertrude Hum's.

MIKE: I want to throw a window pole at something. I want to break a window pane.

AMY: That's because Janet isn't as clever as you'd like her to be.

MIKE: Perhaps. Or because I don't want to go in there to teach.

AMY: You'd better. You said it was your job.

MIKE: Are you all right, Amy?

AMY: I'm always all right. That's the trouble with me. I don't seem able to know what's troubling the others. Something is.

(SECRETARY passes. MIKE goes away. JANET appears.)

AMY: Janet, I wonder if I could speak to you.

JANET: I'm going to see Dr Cornwallis, Mrs Selkirk, I don't want you to tell me what you think of my chances until I've done that.

AMY: I must try to help you, Janet.

JANET: But not yet, please.

(MIKE appears again.)

MIKE: What do you really want to do, Janet. That's the only thing that matters.

AMY: Mr Macalpine, this is my job. Please don't get yourself involved.

MIKE: I am involved.

AMY: Please go and teach.

JANET: I want to be a teacher, Mrs Selkirk, and I know that puts you in a difficult position so I'll leave you and go to see the Headmaster.

(She goes away.)

AMY: It puts me in an impossible position. However, she seems to understand.

MIKE: In your position I think I'd shoot myself.

SMALL BOY: Can we have the window open, please?

MIKE: Yes. I'll do it.

(AMY's voice is heard over as she stands uncertainly.)

I hated English because the exercise books were brown and I took up French because of the smell of coffee. I enjoy life even when it's unsatisfactory. None of my daily failures makes me despair.

AMY (aloud): It's not entirely true. But I don't think I feel as much as I should.

(A smash. She turns.)

MIKE (entering with a window pole): Mrs Selkirk, will you tell the caretaker I've broken a window?

AMY: Do you feel better?

MIKE: Temporarily.

(Enter RAYMOND talking to himself and heading for REG's room.)

RAYMOND: If we are Other men, we must behave as Other men, aloof, stern of purpose,

(He barges into REG's room.)

broad of brow, clear sighted, eyes forever upward and not upon the mere world of mere people, people who are merely mere, pottering about in mereness like moles beneath the endless firmament of knowledge.

(He sits down. AMY leaves.)

SCENE SEVEN

The DEPUTY HEADMASTER's office. REG is standing, RAYMOND is seated.

REG: You forget the protocol by which we live. Stand up in the Deputy Headmaster's room.

RAYMOND (doing so): If you insist.

REG: I do.

RAYMOND: Is this germane?

REG: Indeed it is. To put our house in order we must first admit our place. You are not the Deputy Headmaster.

RAYMOND: I confess I find your attitude –

REG: Sit down!

RAYMOND (doing so): I confess –

REG: Stand up!

RAYMOND (doing so): Your attitude –

REG: Sit down!

RAYMOND (doing so): I find your attitude –

REG: Joyce Pinnington must be worked on.

RAYMOND: Oh. By me?

REG: By you.

RAYMOND: But she's a fool.

REG: Don't pop at me! You'll work on her!

RAYMOND: But why?

REG: She's in love with the Headmaster.

RAYMOND: What?

REG: And you must win her to yourself so that he sees his staunchest ally disappear.

RAYMOND: But I'm engaged!

REG: So?

RAYMOND: What?

REG: Surely it isn't irksome if your duty leads a certain way.

RAYMOND: You make this very sordid.

REG (exploding): Words! Your hurl them about like rocks! I don't expect aspersions of that kind in this room! Oh no!

RAYMOND: But to seduce Joyce Pinnington –

REG: I never said anything of that kind, and I will deny it till my dying day. You will persuade Joyce Pinnington to wear a gown and then befriend Joe Johnson.

RAYMOND (appalled): Joyce Pinnington and Joe Johnson?

REG: You'll work upon their minds until they feel they're naked without gowns, while I approach the Head.

RAYMOND: You'll try an ultimatum?

REG: What?

RAYMOND: I'll leave unless he orders gowns.

REG (one dry laugh): Hah! You really think he cares?

RAYMOND (surprised): Yes.

REG: He'd be glad to see you go. But if I have to use a minatory tone, I shall perhaps imply that I might hand in my resignation.

RAYMOND: I see.

REG: So, Raymond. That's our plan of campaign. At last. You'll kindly take up the two loyalties I've sketched for you and refrain from saying anything that could be construed in any way at all. Then I think you'll find this school will become an academy of which we can be justly proud.

RAYMOND: Yes, Deputy Headmaster. And incidentally, I have a present for you.

REG: I have no offices to sell, Raymond –

RAYMOND: Drawing pins. From the Senior Mistress's desk.

(Both laugh and leave the room together.)

SCENE EIGHT

DAVID is leafing through plans on his desk.

DAVID: The drama block, the library extension, the swimming pool, the running track,

(A knock at the door.)

Come in, the pavillion,

(JANET comes in.)

the extra tennis courts, the computer room, the audio visual centre – sometimes I feel they left out everything except this study.

JANET: It's my career again, sir.

DAVID: Oh, God.

JANET: D'you think I'll make a good teacher?

DAVID: No.

JANET: Why not?

DAVID: You're too attractive. What chance have you got at A level?

JANET: Nobody thinks I've any chance, but if as you said it's character that counts...

(DAVID looks away.)

I'm taking extra tuition in every subject.

DAVID: Well, someone must feel you've some sort of chance.

JANET: They're all men. Mrs Selkirk says I haven't a hope in hell.

DAVID: Did you like Mr Johnson?

JANET: He tries. When is Simpson going to get his lid back?

DAVID: Soon.

JANET: He was very sorry about your having to take it. He's very fond of you.

DAVID: Sit down, Janet. Listen, I failed Simpson. I failed him because I didn't know how to begin doing anything else. I took his lid because it was the only thing I knew how to do. And now he's innocent. Appallingly innocent.

JANET: Do you get enough sleep?

DAVID: No.

JANET: Do you worry in bed?

DAVID: Worry hangs over me like a cloud all day and enters into my mind at night. A hundred little bothers swimming freely round by brain. Absolutely freely, Janet, because I don't know which one to go after first. Look at these plans. Which one should I be pressing ahead with?

Which feature am I most likely to miss, because that's
the most agonising worry of all, that I can't trust myself to see everything there is to see.

JANET: You should be married and share your worries
with your wife.

DAVID: And have her share her worries with me, too?
Oh no. And then again, I'd have to save my energies
for sex. It wouldn't just be holidays, you know, because
what's right is right - I mean a man and wife in bed,
I'd have to do it, and I get so tired, Janet, so tired,
and I need my sleep, and what with children, children
waking up and breakfast time, and coming home there'd
be no time to worry and I'd worry over that and whether
I was right to have them, not being paternal and the
world being as it is.

And then they'd want to come here, wouldn't they? I
mean, if I had so little faith in this place that I didn't
send my own children, that's what everyone would say,
and people can be beastly if you're in authority, so
what's the point of bringing children into such a world,
where people kill and steal? Joe Johnson doesn't kill,
and really he's a very fine man, but are my children
going to know that? are yours? Will you take the risk
of having children when they might be killed by God knows
what, or worse, or have a music master steal their bi-
cycles?

What'll Reg Parsons say when he finds out? There'll be
a row, Janet, and I'll be found with this lid in my room,
and the governors will want to know why Simpson was
allowed to take the thing, and you say I should marry!
Miss Pinnington, I suppose!

JANET: Oh no!

DAVID: What's wrong with her? There's nothing wrong
with Joyce and I appointed her and I should know, but
oh no, people say she's foolish, just because I have
a meal with her occasionally, as if a man can go without the help of feminine society. I need a woman just
as you need Simpson, but the older generation say that
kids like you should know a damn sight better, coming
from a school like this. And what am I supposed to do
all week-end? Snoop and see you don't go too far?

(Pause.)

I tell you, Janet, war's a dreadful thing, and children shouldn't be born to parents who don't realise it, and what with motor accidents, as well –

(Pause.)

Plato was right. Teachers should have mistresses and servants and secretaries and no wives. Plato was absolutely right.

JANET: Yes.

DAVID: You've read Plato?

JANET: No, but I've heard of him, I think.

DAVID: You should read him. You'd enjoy him, Janet, though Aristotle's more difficult. I've tried to live up to the Ethics of Aristotle but I've failed. That's the truth of it. I've failed.   /

You'd better take the lid.

JANET: So all that about needing character to be a teacher wasn't true.

(REG and RAYMOND arrive outside DAVID's office.)

DAVID: Oh, yes, it was true. But we haven't discussed what kind of character, have we?

JANET: Will you recommend me if I get my 'A' levels?

DAVID: Yes.

JANET: Then I'll take the lid.

(They both hold it a second. He lets go.)

DAVID: That's that then.

(He opens the door to let her out.)

DAVID: Ah!

RAYMOND: Oh!

DAVID: Raymond? Can Reg be far behind?

(REG comes forward sliding past RAYMOND into the room. RAYMOND slides back.)

REG: Headmaster.

DAVID: Mr Parsons, you wanted to see me.

REG: It was good of you to make time. I hadn't thought you would take the trouble to...

DAVID: Janet has been asking me if she should become a teacher.

REG (smiling): She would make a delightful contribution to the profession in her personal capacities, Headmaster, but I don't know enough of her intellectual achievements to be able to advance a balanced judgement, I'm afraid.

DAVID: Well, Janet. I've given you my answer. You may go. Please give the lid to Simpson.

JANET: Thank you, sir.

DAVID: Goodbye.

(To RAYMOND):

If you're coming in, do so. Don't lurk.

(RAYMOND comes in. DAVID sits.)

REG: The lid, I take it, was the one Harcourt intends to use as the basis for –

DAVID: When are you going to retire?

REG: What?

DAVID: How old are you?

REG: Forty-three.

DAVID: Seventeen years. How awful.

REG: Dr Cornwallis, I have a serious complaint to register from common room which I feel must be met at once.

DAVID: I wonder if I should've told her not to be a teacher?

REG: It concerns gowns.

DAVID: She's only seventeen.

REG: Common room requires gowns to be worn.

DAVID: Reg – do you know anything about disposal bins for girls?

REG: Not – no. Here is a notice for you to sign.

DAVID: What?

(REG reads one copy, DAVID the other.)

REG: First, that this is an institution whose major duty is to raise the respect for learning to the highest attainable level. Second, that the loyalty you owe to your colleagues requires that you wear the badges of authority where they can be seen, admired, and known for what they are. Third, you have decided that unless you set an example yourself those colleagues in common room whose manners and stature fall somewhat below the standards the profession has come to expect of its fellows, will never attain those standards as long as they are in the school.

DAVID (wearily): Yes, yes, yes, yes, yes.

(With a pen offered by RAYMOND he signs.)

Joe Johnson's leaving, you know. He's a kleptomaniac.

REG and RAYMOND: Yes, yes, yes, yes, yes.

REG (picking up the notice): Thank you, Headmaster.

(RAYMOND and REG leave.)

SCENE NINE

The staff common room. MIKE is there. JOE comes in. SHEILA is outside lying down.

JOE: Mike?

MIKE: Sorry about all this, Joe.

JOE: Yes? Yes. I'll manage. I'm going into business. I shall miss you.

MIKE: Thanks.

JOE: That PE girl. I'm lusting after her again.

MIKE: Steady.

JOE: Don't you lust after her?

MIKE: Yes.

JOE: Then why steady me and not steady you?

MIKE: It's not easy to accept what's been happening.

JOE: I suppose I must try to make it easy, then, even for you.

MIKE: <u>Even</u> for me?

JOE: You're my friend. There's always been supposed to be a sympathy between us.

MIKE: Yes. Well, there is, isn't there?

JOE: Yes. I hope there is. Harcourt's been very kind.

MIKE: I'm surprised.

JOE: You would be. I'm leaving at once so it won't be difficult for you after this afternoon. I'm going north to make my millions.

MIKE: Oh.

JOE: You don't think I can.

MIKE: You aren't the type.

JOE: I might be a financial wizard.

MIKE: No. You and I are ordinary people. We're not clever enough to be financial wizards.

JOE: I'd like to be. I'd like to be able to talk to you. I don't think I've ever really permitted it. I've followed what I believe to be my standards and they haven't got me very far.

MIKE: Your standards are very rigorous. I'm sure they'll stand you in good stead. Joe? Joe?

(JOE has gone out. MIKE goes over to the door. SHEILA comes in.)

Hullo. Aren't you supposed to be supervising something?

(SHEILA shuts the door and looks inviting.)

Are you expecting me to kiss you?

SHEILA: No kissing. I'll be ready in my room in five minutes, Fascist.

MIKE: Isn't this a bit abrupt?

SHEILA: Five minutes should give you time to adjust.

(She goes out of the ordinary door. MIKE looks at his watch. Then he puts his head outside.)

MIKE: Joe? Are you all right?

(No sign of JOE.)

Five minutes then.

(He smiles. RAYMOND bursts in.)

RAYMOND: Right. You're the first. Gowns are to be statutory from now on. We have brought our influence to bear and our influence has proved not inconsiderable. Now I think you'll find professional standards will return to this God-forsaken academy of ours. When they do, I think we may expect to see a very different school, a very different school indeed.

MIKE: A rather darker one, apparently.

RAYMOND: Your facetiousness, Macalpine, is what strikes me as typifying the puerility of this staff.

(MIKE appears preoccupied.)

What's the matter?

MIKE: I'm going to have the PE mistress in four minutes' time.

RAYMOND: Do you mean 'have' in the argot sense of the word?

MIKE: Yes.

RAYMOND: I say. How d'you know?

MIKE: She told me.

RAYMOND: Gosh.

MIKE: If I take it slowly I'll just about get there. Really, things turn out quite nicely on occasions.

RAYMOND: Just a minute. Is this exclusive?

MIKE: I don't imagine so.

RAYMOND: She's thick as two short planks.

MIKE: Aren't you engaged?

RAYMOND: We all have imaginations, you know.

MIKE: I'll make enquiries on your behalf.

RAYMOND: No. I had a nasty experience once at Cambridge. It all seemed right, the sported oak, the aphrodisiac muffins, the mystery of the damp, collegiate evening.

(MIKE has gone.)

Blast you then.

(Enter HARCOURT.)

HARCOURT: Ah, Raymond. You're teaching in the sixth form prep. room, I see.

RAYMOND: Gowns are to be statutory clothing from now on, Harcourt. What d'you think of that?

HARCOURT: They keep the chalk off your clothing, I suppose, and regulations always occupy the minds of one's colleagues who might otherwise interfere in matters of importance.

(Enter HARRY CLOPTON, furious.)

HARRY: There are two bloody classes in this school at the moment without teachers, and they are both supposed to be having English.

RAYMOND: May I suggest that the Science Department minds it's own business as far as the teaching of English is concerned?

HARRY: If the English I receive in my science books is typical, no.

RAYMOND: If your subject were made interesting enough to capture the minds of those you teach —

HARRY: If the standard of English in this school depended upon the interest generated in your classes —

RAYMOND: This has nothing to do with the science department, whose unwarranted interference —

HARRY: You are stealing from the taxpayer. If I were Head, you'd go.

HARCOURT: The English my form is doing can be done as well without me as with me. There's not much point in teaching most of it. Those lessons which I do conduct as you very properly suggest I should are quite different. My classes know this and until the world runs differently this is how it will be. As for Raymond, it's almost worth paying him to stay away from the school altogether.

RAYMOND: That's not the kind of leadership one looks for in the Head of a department.

(JOYCE appears with a tambourine.)

HARRY: Oh no!...This is ridiculous...Is there anybody teaching English at the moment?

JOYCE: I'm free.

HARRY: Oh, are you?...Are you...I'd like this to be understood. We're in this school to impart knowledge and to do so in person. I shall report the increasing laxity in this matter to anyone who will listen.

JOYCE: Oh, will you. Then you might as well know that I shall mention certain attitudes towards the PE department which can be made to sound pretty sensational.

HARRY: Personal matters are not relevant, and anyway it was a joke.

JOYCE: Pretty sensational.

HARRY: All right, then. All right. I hope your conscience is clear on that, Joyce. I hope you don't mind the taxpayer being robbed. Because that's what it is.

(He goes out. HARCOURT goes with him.)

RAYMOND: Well done, Joyce.

(He leers.)

Won't you sit down?

(She does so, rather surprised.)

Joyce, I've noticed – pardon me if I seem impertinent – I've noticed that you don't always seem very happy here. Am I right?

JOYCE: Yes.

RAYMOND: I'd like to alter that.

(JOYCE very surprised. He kneels.)

It's a question of attitude, isn't it?

JOYCE: Raymond, I find that remark unbelievable and if you'll pardon me for appearing rude –

(She gets up.)

RAYMOND: Sit down! Please, Joyce.

JOYCE: I don't want to discuss my attitude with you of all people, Raymond.

RAYMOND (pulling her down into her chair): It's not your attitude I'm thinking about, Joyce, it's the attitude of others. The small people who have lost the flavour of

Parnassus. Between us, we can establish it again.

(He holds her hand.)

I can make you happy, Joyce, today. Will you wear your gown? There's a directive about it coming from the Head, but you and I, Joyce, we can give immeasurable help by wearing our gowns with joy.

JOYCE: Gowns?

RAYMOND: We must get them all to wear their gowns, be missionaries together in his name. The Deputy Headmaster and myself decided to approach you, knowing how you felt towards Dr Cornwallis. We thought you'd like to help in this.

JOYCE: You silly young man.

RAYMOND: I hardly merit these insults from everyone!

(He gets up.)

JOYCE (near tears): Well, you do from me. Go and teach the sixth form who are fighting in their prep. room, and stop wasting everybody's time.

(He marches to the door.)

RAYMOND: Bitch!

(He marches out. The bell goes. He marches back again.)

The lesson's over.

JOYCE: I heard the bell.

RAYMOND: Where's the tea?

JOYCE: It's late.

RAYMOND: Everything's late in this place.

(There is an awkward silence. Behind their backs. outside the staff room, JOE can be seen setting up a step ladder and throwing a noosed rope round some overhang. HARCOURT suddenly pushes in the tea trolley, followed by the noisily chattering staff. The SMALL BOY appears near JOE. From the ladder JOE tries to kick him away. The staff collect their tea in the midst of chatter and noise, as REG and RAYMOND appear.

As REG addresses the assembled staff we can see JOE behind him, arguing with the SMALL BOY. After some

minutes, the SMALL BOY runs out and appears in the
staff room at the appropriate place. When he goes, JOE
slips and swings stupidly by his arms, and eventually
falls heavily to the ground, hurting himself. He then
limps into the staff room at the appropriate place.)

REG: May I have silence, ladies and gentlemen before
you depart? I want to draw attention to the Headmaster's
new ordinance that we should all in future wear gowns.
You may well feel that this decision has been taken
without the full consent of common room in the usual
manner, but in fact many soundings have been taken and
a chart of your general feelings has been prepared in
what I think must be considered a reasoned and carefully assessed way. Of course, the final decision in
matters like this lies with the Headmaster. Now, whatever I say here is, of course in the strictest confidence,
and I know you will observe that high tradition we have
pioneered in respect of dirty linen.

(Crash as JOE falls off ladder.)

The association between the outbreak of stealing in the
school and those who do not wear gowns might fairly be
described as the last straw on a very long suffering back.

SMALL BOY (arriving): Sir!

REG: And the Headmaster has reluctantly felt compelled to
order gowns to be worn.

SMALL BOY: Sir, Mr Johnson's hanging himself.

REG: Who let this boy into common room?

SMALL BOY: Sir, he is!

REG: It is a principle of teaching and one that I am constantly affirming that whatever is done in common room
is done in camera.

(JOE has limped in.)

JOYCE (holding a tambourine): Joe? Are you all right?

JOE: I think so.

JOYCE: Come and have a cup of tea.

JOE: I don't think tea will be enough, Joyce.

JOYCE (leading him to it): Nonsense. You need a cup of tea.

(Everyone is looking at JOYCE and JOE, she still with her tambourine.)

REG (furious): You see how it is, Raymond? He has quite deliberately spoiled the impact of my announcement. It is hard to believe that such malicious people exist.

CURTAIN

Methuen's Modern Plays

EDITED BY JOHN CULLEN

Max Frisch	THE FIRE RAISERS ANDORRA
Jean Giraudoux	TIGER AT THE GATES DUEL OF ANGELS
Rolf Hochhuth	THE REPRESENTATIVE
Heinar Kipphardt	IN THE MATTER OF J. ROBERT OPPENHEIMER
Arthur Kopit	CHAMBER MUSIC and other plays
Jakov Lind	THE SILVER FOXES ARE DEAD and other plays
Henry Livings	KELLY'S EYE and other plays EH?
John Mortimer	THE JUDGE
Joe Orton	CRIMES OF PASSION LOOT WHAT THE BUTLER SAW
Harold Pinter	THE BIRTHDAY PARTY THE ROOM and THE DUMB WAITER THE CARETAKER A SLIGHT ACHE and other plays THE COLLECTION and THE LOVER THE HOMECOMING TEA PARTY and other plays LANDSCAPE and SILENCE
Jean–Paul Sartre	CRIME PASSIONNEL
Theatre Workshop and Charles Chilton	OH WHAT A LOVELY WAR